THE VOICES PROJECT:
ALL GOOD THINGS

A Long Walk Home by Yarrie Bangura

Lazlo's Feet by Michael J. Cornford

Coast by Alberto Di Troia

Teeth by Piri Eddy

Scrub by Georgia Goode

Changing Room by C.J. McLean

The Fuzz by Kirby Medway

Nice by Gemma Neall

Red Bull by Rachel O'Regan

Possession by Morgan St. Clair

Bright by Ciella Williams

Currency Press
Sydney

ATYP
Australian Theatre
for Young People

CURRENCY PLAYS

First published in 2016
by Currency Press Pty Ltd,
PO Box 2287, Strawberry Hills, NSW, 2012, Australia
enquiries@currency.com.au
www.currency.com.au

in association with Australian Theatre for Young People.

FOREWORD

CIELLA WILLIAMS

So much of being a teenager is about wanting to leave.

I was desperate to get out of high school. I couldn't wait to go travelling. I couldn't wait to get out of this smelly, humid little town and into the bright lights (read: grey drizzle) of Melbourne.

I've never felt more euphoric than on the last day of high school. I danced for hours on concrete lunch tables in thirty-four degrees heat, wrapped in bandages (my muck-up-day costume was a Sexy Mummy), because this was it! I was getting out!

Leaving is monumental to a seventeen-year-old. When I was told that this year's National Studio theme was 'departures', I thought of the departure from innocence. I say 'departure' because I don't think it's a loss. It's a movement—from ignorance to awareness.

Departures are also discoveries. We learn to inhabit new knowledge when we leave a version of ourselves behind.

At first I struggled with the monologue form. It seemed hard to justify seven minutes of talking from one person. Out loud. I now see it as a perfect way to express some of the intensely personal moments of growing up.

Every writer in this group has captured a critical moment of departure in each of their pieces. Whether it's the untimely death of a lover or a character coming to terms with feminist thought, there's no going back for any of these characters.

The opportunity to meet other young playwrights and established writers from around the country has caused a massive shift in my thinking. Maybe I can write! I've certainly gone from feeling creatively isolated to having a network of peers (and friends) around the country. And although all good things must come to an end, I have a feeling that there will be more good things to come.

Ciella Williams is a Darwin-based writer and performer. She attended the 2015 ATYP National Studio and her piece, *Bright,* is included in this publication.

Darius Williams learning lines for TEETH by Piri Eddy.

CONTENTS

Rehearsals for All Good Things.

INTRODUCTION

IAIN SINCLAIR

The wonderful thing about monologues is that you get to step into the eye of someone's mind. You get access to information most normal human beings would never dream of sharing. You get to meet the deep, innermost 'them'. There's something about the intimacy of a monologue that draws the audience and the speaker into a trusting relationship that almost never happens in day-to-day life. The speaker entrusts you with the most extraordinary internal impulses that range from the disturbing and dark, to the achingly tender and beautiful, right through to stuff that is just downright bonkers.

I still remember my first encounter with a dedicated monologue in live performance, it blew my tiny mind at the time: I was watching a production of Othello in the park when a man called Iago, a seemingly affable and keen-to-help kind of guy, waved off his friend Roderigo with a warm smile and then suddenly turned, looked directly at me and said, 'Thus do I ever make my fool my purse'. I remember thinking, 'Did that man just confess his evil mind to me? Why on earth would he do that?' Iago went on… 'For I mine own gain'd knowledge should profane if I would time expend with such a snipe. But for my sport and profit. I hate the Moor.' This man just straight-out revealed his horrible secret intent to me and the whole park! What was I supposed to do with that information? I wanted to turn to the people next to me and say, 'This man needs to be stopped!'… but I didn't. Instead I found myself compelled by the confidence he put in me, and to my shame by the end of the play a hidden part of my own soul could even be said to have been barracking for this out-and-out rascal.

Of course, dedicated monologues can reveal so much more than an evil-minded pursuit of 'sport and profit' and this volume is testimony to that. The voices we hear in All Good Things range across a vast spectrum of the Australian teenage experience from what races through your mind when you go completely blank in a final examination, to the giant internal agonies of unrequited love, the great yearning to get to brighter lights and bigger things, the challenges of being born male in a female body in the suburbs, right through to the return of that ancient and cruel rite of passage relating to young men and facial hair (yeah, thanks a lot hipsters).

When I was seventeen, my mother and I tried very hard to understand each other and failed. I can still see her on the verge of tears in the kitchen saying to me, 'If only I could see inside your mind, love, but I can't!' If only I could have handed her a copy of a play script like this. It would have gone a long way to helping her understand the colossal mysteries and passions that I was wrangling with at the time.

These eleven young Australian voices privilege us into the astonishingly complex, sensitive yet robust workings of seventeen-year-old minds from all walks of life across Australia now. It is brave and magnificent writing and it reveals so much more about the bright dreams, dark horrors and massive artistic ambitions of the next generation. It is a volume that every politician, teacher and parent should read and, above all, it is a collection of intimate conversations that young Australians can have with themselves, for their own private, mysterious and awesome reasons.

Iain Sinclair is a director, dramaturg and translator with a strong interest in new writing.

All Good Things was first produced by the Australian Theatre for Young People premiering at Studio 1, The Wharf, Sydney, on 3 February 2016, with the following cast:

Bright	Poppy Lynch
The Fuzz	Jonas Thompson
Coast	Simon Croker
Teeth	Darius Williams
Nice	Sarah Meacham
Red Bull	May Tran
Changing Room	Moreblessing Maturure
Scrub	Simone Cheuanghane
Possession	Alex Packard
Lazlo's Feet	Martin Hoggart

Director, Iain Sinclair
Assistant Director, Lucy Clements
Sound Designer, Michael Toisuta
Lighting Designer, Emma Lockhart-Wilson
Set & Costume Designer, Emma Vine
Dramaturg, Jennifer Medway
Stage Manager, Michael Cornford
Production Manager, Juz McGuire

Day one of the National Studio 2015 with all twenty playwrights.

A LONG WALK HOME

YARRIE BANGURA

Writer's note: This piece is not autobiographical. The writer hopes that it might give a voice to people taking refuge in Australia from unrest in their country of origin.

People tell us in Australia there will not be African food. They repeat it over and over, there will be no rice to eat. No stew. There will be no rice to eat. The day we leave we eat as much as we can, especially me, I eat so much it is as if I am pregnant.

My grandmother, my aunty, all my relatives come to the airport to say goodbye. 'If we don't see you again, that's it, goodbye.' 'We'll see you again in the next world.' 'Please don't forget us.'

They tell me Australia is the last continent and it's surrounded by water. Where can I run to there? I can't even swim. I am scared the sharks will eat me.

I go to school. In my traditional clothes. At the school they ask me so many questions, about my hairstyle braid twist. 'Where do you come from?' 'Why did you come here?' 'What was it like there?' 'Did you live among the animals?' 'Did you live in a tree?'

Seriously?

My house was two stories, next to the ocean. Surrounded by green. My house was so fancy that you could go to the bus stop and ask them for the yellow house.

I had everything at my fingertips
Shofel driving me to school, my friend's house to play
My parents have plenty of money
They were generous givers to whoever was in need
'I want braids, Conrad braids, twists… I like twists'
Whatever I, princess, feels like
Love was all I saw
Happy faces all around

Beautiful vibrant colours
Every day is a celebration
We dance, we sing.
Everybody is my family.
Every night in the village we bless the moon
[*Singing maybe in Susu*] 'I see the moon, the moon sees me,
God bless the moon and God bless me.'
In the village there's no TV.
We dance till we're tired. We form a group down the hill and
up the hill, come together to meet in a village choir. We have
the instrument players. The boys. Our elders sit down to watch
us and cheer for us. We sing with joy and laughter. Stomping
our feet to the ground. The red dust arises. We dance with
deep-meaning songs. Song of joy, song of sadness. Some
of them are sad. But every song has steps. Like sometimes
the dance is like a competition as well. The dance becomes
a competition like battle. Whoever shakes it the most wins.
And we end with stories from our elders. Stories just like the
Dreamtime.
It all sounds like a beautiful life.
'Where do you come from?' 'Why did you come here?'
My school is a private school. Very secure facility with
bodyguards. No-one can come to collect a child except if the
parents give permission.
We are at school when we hear a loud sound, *bam! bam!* Our
teacher, Mrs Kamar, is shaking and confused. There is no time
for questions and the school gate is wide open for the first
time. We all run out of the school gate and people are falling,
crying, shouting, pushing. Tear gas explodes, like chilli in my
eyes.
It is the beginning of war in my country, Sierra Leone. The
rebels did this. Hands, legs chopped off and victims left
in pools of blood, houses burnt, properties lost, gunshots
everywhere, children abandoned and crying for their parents.
At the end of that first day the street is empty and quiet like
the graveyard, animals silent in the street, heavy smoke from
the guns and the houses on fire. The only voices are the rebels
and their loud music. Rejoicing.

They take young people as hostages. They go from door to door, banging and forcing the door open. They yell, 'Open this door now or we burn you alive!' They take young boys and convert them into rebels. They take young girls and to them they do awful things. They took me. They take us to a house far away from our families. They keep us there. To young girls they do awful things.

It's all confusing to my mind. Who are these people? The monsters that want to swallow us? This is not my family.

'Where do you come from?' 'Why did you come here?'

We survive. We reach the border. We travel to Conakry, the city. But we are not allowed to enter the city. The Guineans they are scared of us, they take us far, far away, they don't know if we are rebels in disguise or if we are seeking refuge so they take us far, far away.

They take us to Kayla Camp. People in uniforms, faces different colour, different skin to me, they give us tents, groundnut oil, bulghur, maize and a grey blanket, and for a moment I feel joy. I feel safe.

But the camp is not safe. The rebels come from Sierra Leone to Kayla Camp. They attack the camp and we run from bullets to wild animals. They are here. They have come again. Panicking, panicking again, I cannot think. I hide. The Guinean army is strong, they push the rebels away. I am living but I am not living. I am here but I am not here.

Flying over Australia I see blackness. Where is the land? Then I see lights twinkling like bright multi-coloured stars all over the ground. I am so scared, my heart is beating fast, my hands wet from sweating, my mind in turmoil: what is this upside down country with stars on the ground? I squeeze my mother's hand. The plane gets faster and lower, until *boom!* *bang!* like gunfire, and we are among the coloured lights on the ground.

I thanked God that my feet would soon be on the ground. I am pushed through a bright white tunnel. The plane is giving birth to me and depositing me into a new world. This new world inside is full of bright lights, but outside I can see a familiar darkness. Strange to have night and day next to each other. This bright glass-walled terminal building is as big as two villages back home. All the brick houses and mud huts and all the villagers could fit inside. My startled eyes look up at the ceiling lights so much, so much I nearly lose my balance. I feel like it is going to swallow me. Colours and noises swirl, people smile at me, Indians, Chinese, Polynesians and white people all smiling at me. Then I saw them! Africans! My uncle and his family waiting to take us home. My uncle looks fatter and richer, maybe Australia is a good place. He came to the airport to pick us up in his car. A car! We all piled into the car—packed like foliage in the scrub. I am wide-eyed at everything around me. The smells and noises none familiar to me. We drive through the night towards my uncle's house. So many cars and bright lights along the way. My head starts to hurt again, my thoughts about the war and a safe place to hide here confused. Where are the open spaces? There are houses and buildings everywhere. Where are the places to run to?

We arrive at my uncle's house and he opens the door. A familiar smell comes to me, a smell from home. Food! A feast all set out for our arrival. Foods from home! The first night in my uncle's house was a wondrous night. The house was full of modern gadgets that had so many different uses. How could they need so many things? Back home a knife, a *matapensu* and some wooden bowls were all we needed. But here, so many useless and confusing things. The light switch! I must have stood for fifteen minutes flicking the switch, watching the light go on and off, on and off, on and off. How powerful I felt, that this was under my control.

My mum told me Australia is a new life. A new home. A better life. A life that I once lived is reborn. How is this possible when I can't speak their language, when I can't read? Then I saw the most amazing sight on TV, a beautiful black woman. That all the white people in the audience stood and cheered for. I asked my uncle who this woman was. My uncle told me she was a very rich and well-educated woman from America, who did a lot of good things for many people all over the world. Her name was Oprah. I was stunned to see a black woman who held so many people in one. She spoke so well with no African accent and she seemed so smart and wise. I was reformed. 'Where is she from?' I also had that question. I thought Opera

4

House was Oprah's house. That it was named after her. I thought she might have been a refugee. I wanted to know more about this woman. I wanted to be like her, a strong, smart black woman who could change lives.

I stand in front of the mirror pretending like the cameras are in front of me taking pictures of me. I am blushing with a big smile. With very white shining teeth and bright red lipstick, people all round me with smiling and happy faces. Tick, flash, action, camera.

'Where do you come from?' 'Why did you come here?'
Ripped from my homeland like an unrooted tree
Transplanted to a new land
Here I took root
The lingering sufferance from my homeland
Severed limbs scattered
Like jagged, discarded branches
I stand on blood-soaked earth
My feet caked in gore
Frantic with horror
Running into the arms of Aunty Australia
Scattering seeds from Mama Africa
The earth is cool and green
The waterlily shoots from the mud.

▼ ▼ ▼ ▼ ▼

LAZLO'S FEET

MICHAEL J. CORNFORD

DAVID stands beside the trunk of a large, old gum tree. He is next to a pair of boots.

People call me Fordy.
See, I'm the fourth David in my family.
David Malcolm White—the fourth.
The fourth D… Four-D.

> *He sighs.*

Soon as I hit eighteen next month, I'm changing it. Anything else—James. I like James—James, first of his name.

We live in the Glen.
It's a dry spot.
We're waiting for rain a lot at home.
Got to do a lot to make up for it.
Spend a lot to keep afloat.
Makes getting away tough.
Economy's hard, you know.

Had this school trip to Sydney last year though.
Saw the Powerhouse Museum, saw the bridge and the Opera House, but the best thing was just the city itself.
It didn't matter where you were there was always something to do, see, eat, root… All of the above.

I couldn't tell you how long I was just staring out at the water.

Can't get over how big the ocean is, you know?

> *Pause.*

So, we got to pick our 'buddies' that we had to keep an eye out for during the trip.

Well, my buddy's always been Lazlo.

When you're out here and the nearest person of your own age lives kilometres away, you just kind of have to be stuck with what you've got.

Pause.

Can't be far off without his boots.

Pause.

Dad says, *Lion King* style, 'Look, Fordy. Everything the fence line touches, all this, is our property. When my time comes, all this will be yours.'

But what if I don't want it?

He doesn't hear me.

'And your kids will have it, and theirs too, if God's good. We all shuffle off eventually. But this land. This is ours.'

Pause.

I didn't ask for it. I don't want it. I don't want any of this.

Lazlo and me, we've made up our minds.

We need to be in the city.

Out of the dry and near the water.

I've got my car, and some money put away from Gran's inheritance.

I'll work in a café or some shit and Lazlo can do pretty much anything, he's so great—top of our class.

Exams have finally fucked off and we can just *go*.

We'll get some shitty rental, anywhere easy to get to the beach.

We'll take our shirts off and kick off our boots—Lazlo will pull me into the waves.

We'll be happy. We'll be free. Barefoot and I'm me.

So right now I'm waiting for him at the spot we usually duck wire to meet.
A huge gum tree, standing alone above these fields of tall amber grasses.
They've overgrown—died off.
But the remains are still towering higher than me, higher than anyone I know.

DAVID looks down to the boots in his hands.

His boots are here.

This tree's been here a long time.

It's old.

I wonder if the past Davids in my family knew it. If they came here. Saw it when it was younger.

Pause.

Did they like who they were? Were they all just the same?
I remember Dad telling me about how the first David got himself bit by a Brown.

Nasty way to go.

Where's Lazlo?

I can see his roof from here. Green Colorbond steel. The old one fell in…
Well…
His dad strung himself up.
Bad choice of beam. It wasn't the rope that got him. It was the roof falling in.

Lazlo… His eyes changed after that. Like they'd grown older.

New roof now.
Lazlo did a lot of the work putting it up, he's real easy with heights.

Pause.

Not up in our tree now though.

Pause.

The air seems to shift.

A stark black crow dives down from somewhere high up in the tree, down into the thick grasses. Out of sight.

The light's changing, we should have left by now.

Pause.

Come on, Lazlo. I thought I mattered.

> *DAVID circles the tree, looking out while inhaling deeply and exhaling. Circling the tree, he stares out. Deeply inhales. Pause. Deeply exhales. He looks at the boots in his hand.*

Where the fuck is Lazlo?!

> *He traces the bark with his hand.*

Just there.

That's where Lazlo pressed his head nervously when he told me he liked me.

Here was where he stood when I held his hand for our first kiss.

And here,

here is where he held me after my gran died.

He held me so fucking long.

Two more crows drop.

Caw. Squawk. Caw.

Three crows having a blue.

I take one step into the grass and a crow takes off and shoots right above me.

His eyes follow the crow up to the tree. He notices other crows, they are waiting for something. His eyes track what the crows are looking at. He sees Laszlo.

Lazlo's feet.

DAVID places the boots down at the foot of the tree and, while sitting, addresses them.

I find that I…
Like a lot…
Just stare…
Looking at nothing to find something. Some meaning for it all.
You were the only one that made me feel—

Pause.

Like I wasn't 'Fordy'. I could actually just be James. That my life wasn't a fucking trap.
That I can be—that I am… me.

He slowly outreaches one hand.

It was right there.
I could…
Touch…

His hand lowers and drops.

No—it's gone…

His gaze rises to the top of the tree.

No matter how beautiful—dead's dead.

▼ ▼ ▼ ▼ ▼

COAST

ALBERTO DI TROIA

*MICHAEL, seventeen, wearing discoloured, tatty board shorts
and a t-shirt with a long-faded print.*

This
awful
shining
pounding
burning
keeps me stuck here,
stuck together,
swells and surges,
breaks.
Gathers.
Sweeps me down the coast,
past the music and the ferris wheel,
lights flashing,
by the jetty, hotels and motels,
to the beach.
Crowds of boys
laughing,
jostling,
muscles under soft skin gleaming,
sweat beading,
tan lines peeling.
They can't see me.
I think I'm invisible.
I don't know.
I've never had the chance
to get close enough
before summer passes.

Now
in winter,
in the ocean,
a boy is swimming
alone
through steel-grey waves.
Muscles ripple,
soft golden skin,
fine brown hair catches light,

swirls round chest,
fades over stomach,
trails into shorts
where it curls round and—
awful
shining
burning
pounding
pushes me
closer.
I watch him from the rocks,
drying off
on the sand—
muscles stretching,

fine hairs swirling—
he's looking right at me.
Walking over.
Must be someone behind me,

He glances behind his shoulder.

there are rocks behind me.

He glances back.

He's putting out his hand,

Coast

I have to take it and
heat
blooms between our palms
shoots straight up my arm,
blurs my vision
my edges flicker
my body shimmers
I'm sure I'll
burn right through him—
[As *'the boy*] 'Ow, your hand is fucking freezing.'

Still as the boy, he takes out a cigarette and lights it.

'Do you live here?'

As MICHAEL, he nods. As the boy:

'Fuck, that's bad luck. I'm down for the weekend. Dad's trying
to sell a house on the beachfront. [*Whispering conspiratorially*]
It's a last-ditch family bonding session.'

As the boy, he throws the cigarette to the floor.

'If you're around, I'm gonna hang out here again tomorrow.
Might see you.'

Next morning
he's out surfing.
I stand knee-deep and watch.
He's not very good,
gets dumped a lot.
Pretends like he means to do it,
waves his arms around,
throws himself off the board,
wetsuit clinging tight
to his back and chest while I
pulse
burn

simmer the water around my legs.
I go stand on the sand before I disappear into a cloud of salty
steam.

His family are the only guests in the nice motel.
From the dark on the bend of the road,
I watch
until the lights go out.

'Nice one. She didn't see shit. Have some popcorn.'
We're the only two people in the old cinema on the main
street.
He made me sneak in while he flirted with the ticket girl.
She wouldn't have noticed anyway.
My leg next to his,
my hand curled near his thigh.
Inch by inch
I rest it against his jeans.
Heat oozes out
immediately
around the backs of my fingers.
I let my leg fall
against his,
wiry brown hairs scrape at my hairless shin,
little hot matchsticks striking on my skin,
ready to erupt into flame
burn through his edges.
I don't dare look at him.
Burning,
I just stare straight ahead at
the shifting blurring curling colours on the screen.

His parents have been fighting all weekend.
'They're gonna get divorced. About fucking time.'
He buries his face in his arm so I can't see him crying.
The ferris wheel groans and creaks around us,
the carriage

swinging
four feet off the ground.
I stare at his legs,
muscles curving up
into shorts where they meet in an
awful
shining—
I reach out
put my hand on his
thigh,
move it
slowly,
burning,
up his—
'Why is your skin always so fucking cold? Are you sick, or
something?'

   Beat.

His leg shifts
towards me.
The smallest movement.
An offer.

   MICHAEL stretches out his hand.

Again
I move
up his leg and
creep
inside
his shorts and
awful
burning
shining
daring me to
lean forward,

burn right through him,
into the ferris wheel,
melt the steel,
buckle and fall,
mush us
into a
mess of bones and flesh—
shaking and clattering,
he gets to his feet.
Leaping down.
'I've gotta go, ah… pack for tomorrow. Sorry dude.'

I wait outside the motel
till he comes out for a smoke then—
'Fuck, you scared the shit out of me! Where did you come
from?'
I show him a bottle.
I stole it for him.
He takes a long
last drag on his cigarette and
flicks it into the dark.

The beach is black
and cold, and wet,
the half-finished bottle
lying on the sand,
next to his shirt.
He's stumbling,
staggering.
We sway around the beach,
awkward slow dance.
His mouth, hot by my ear.
'You wanna fuck me, don't you? 'S'okay man, I don't fucken
care…'
I lean into him,
brush my forehead

Coast

against his.
He giggles,
headbutts me back,
softly;
tries to push me away but
I hold on tight.
Run my mouth along his neck,
shoulders,
my hand burns on his stomach,
slides down his pelvis,
slips into his shorts
past a curly hot wire thicket of hair to—
he's laughing now.
I push at our shorts
push them down and
he's laughing hysterically,
like it's the funniest thing.
I press myself against him,
flat up against him and
the heat shoots up between our bodies like hot glue.
Turn him around,
his back to me and I'm
'You're so fucking cold!'
—a filament burning at highest voltage.

'Argh, you're fucking freezing!'
—I'm not freezing you idiot I'm fucking burning.

He wrestles against me but
I'm strong.
And he's
moaning
or screaming
I can't tell
over the roaring
in my head

17

of fire,
I'm on fire,
burning through him,
scorching his edges
charring and smoking
and falling away
so there's nothing between us
but smoke and air
and heat and flame
so I take my chance
I lean forward
I fall right through
into him
and for a second I am completely inside his body and there's
a thumping thumping thumping and I realise, I remember it's
the sound of a heart pumping and I'm falling for a gasping
heaving millisecond I realise a heart is in my chest and blood
pumping through me and alcohol in the blood and for a
gasping heaving millisecond I remember what it's like but I—
tear out through the front of him and
sprawl face-first onto the sand.

   Pause.

He's standing completely still.
Mouth open.
Smoke wisping off him.
Staring
but not seeing.
Right through me.
He collapses
topples
straight forward.
Thud
facedown in the sand.

It trickles out slowly

Coast

at first,
then surging
gushing
cresting
breaking—
awful
shining
pounding
burning
streaming out of me,
into the sea
till I'm empty.
Still.
My edges flicker
blur
split
fray,
spiral up
into the air,
snatched by the wind
and carried
above the beach
like I was never there
on the sand
beside the naked boy
lying facedown
in the tide.

▼ ▼ ▼ ▼ ▼

TEETH

PIRI EDDY

DANIEL. Seventeen. Standing on the crowded porch after his grandmother's funeral.

I'm standing on the porch.
I'm standing with a beer on the porch because Dad let me have one.
Just this once. And it's hot. I'm standing with a beer on the porch and it's hot. And everyone is talking. Laughing. In Bev's house.
Because of.
It's this shirt. Polyester. This polyester shirt that's hot. It's making me hot. It makes the sweat pool at the base of my back. Dad made me wear it, and his idea of fashion is socks and thongs, so I'm looking about as cool as the bargain bin at an op-shop.
I sip my beer but it's gone warm. And I must pull a face because there's this old bloke standing on the other side of the room. Someone I don't know. Don't think I know him. Looking at me. His mouth tugs a little at the edge. I see the teeth. Even from here I see brown. See that they're sawn off at the bottom. And Brown Teeth comes up to me and says: 'Your grandmother was always so proud of you.'
Hands on my arm.
'Your grandmother,' he says.
With those crooked teeth. Crooked brown teeth. Wrinkled skin.
Everyone keeps saying, 'Your grandmother'. Like they know. And grandmother? Right. When if they *knew* me then they'd *know* I call her Bev. That was our thing.
I slip away from Brown Teeth. People keep looking at me. Smiling at me. The oldies all love my shirt. They want to know what op-shop I got it from. Got to be nice. Dad says you've got

to be nice to old people because it's not their fault they're old.
And you can't do much about the smell. But it's like *Dawn of
the Dead* in here, just with more fake hips.
There's this taste in my throat. Like warm beer. And I feel.
People are looking. Smiling. Sets of teeth. Crooked teeth.
Teeth that might slip out of flapping lips at any second. Dad's
watching me with a sausage roll in his hand. Ketchup on his
chin. Who feels hungry after a funeral? How can you feel
hungry at a time like this? People are looking. With their teeth.
Hands on my arm. Wrinkled skin. The smell.
Sorry. Sorry but I… have to take a…
I'm inside. Kitchen's empty. It's just me and it's quiet. I can
breathe. There's a pavlova sitting on the counter, covered in
strawberries and blueberries. Everyone knows Bev makes the
best pav! World's best. Dead set. This one won't be as good
though. Bev would always have the meringue done before we
came over. But the kids put the blueberries and strawberries
on. And Bev would be running around like crazy.
With the kitchen steaming. Sweating.
Her in the middle of it all.
Crashing. Clanking.
So the rest of us could eat until our stomachs hurt.
I pick up a blueberry. It squishes in my hand and I get juice. I
get blue running down my arm. I wipe it off quick before it
gets on my shirt, because I know Dad would say, 'Brand new
shirt, Daniel!'
And I think—
I think, maybe I'll make a pav like Bev's. With all the good stuff.
Strawberries. Blueberries.
Except…
I dunno how I'd make it. Eggs? Flour? I never asked.
Still got that lump in my throat. I go to the cupboard. For a
drink, maybe. Go to the cupboard but I'm kind of not there and
I'm just opening whatever and then I open this cupboard I've
never opened and there's all these… Just sitting on the shelf.
All these pre-packed meringues on the shelf.
Sitting there waiting to be opened.
Like,

A hundred of them.

I can't help but laugh. World's best pav, right?

Pause.

Dad's still outside by the sausage rolls. I spot him double-parked and chewing a third. Ketchup on his chin. On his shirt. In his teeth.

Now I'm in the lounge and there's a photo tree on the wall. Just a bunch of photos of Bev stuck to the wall.

Like, Instagram for old people.

Black and white, or, sort of brownish. Like Brown Teeth with the sawn-offs. There's Bev smiling. It's nice to see Bev and her smile again.

Then this girl comes up behind me, wearing black. Crying. Or she was. You can see where her make-up has run down her face. She looks my age. Little older maybe, but she's pretty. Like, dead set. So I try to look cool, squint like the movie stars do.

DANIEL pulls a face, like he's smelt something rotten.

But I reckon I must look less like Brad Pitt and more like Sylvester Stallone on a bad day because she gives me this look, like the way you look at someone's ugly baby when you can't actually say it looks ugly.

We don't say anything. I should say something. You're supposed to say things to pretty women, aren't you? I should say something. I shouldn't say anything. I open my mouth and then close it. Open. Close. I'm a bloody fish.

I think.

     I try.

          Something.

               Anything.

It's hot. We're standing there and it's hot with this polyester shirt and I'm sweating. Just standing there. And this girl must see the sweat marks around my pits but at least she doesn't point it out.

Then the girl in black says, 'Bev had such a wonderful life, didn't she?'

And I reply: Yeah, wow!

        Like, real smooth.

I want to melt into goo and slurp away.

And the pretty girl in black says, 'You're Daniel, right? Bev always talked about you. Whenever I'd bring in her tea and stuff.'

I know I should say… like… something, like… I should say something like, 'My reputation precedes me'. And wink, or something. But these pit stains. It's hot. So I just nod. Like, twenty times. Because I'm an idiot.

Maybe she's noticed how much I'm sweating except she still doesn't mention it which is nice. Then I spot a photo of an older lady I don't know. Bev's mum or something, and before I can stop myself there's my mouth opening. Not closing.

Opening.

And I say, 'Who's that?', before I realise.

That's her. That's Bev. Brown teeth, wrinkled skin.

Looking tired.

Old.

Like she could actually.

And the pretty girl in black who didn't point out that I was sweating real bad just looks at me, and I think I must have pulled that face again. And there is…

        silence.

I need…

fresh air.

I'm out the door leading to the garden, away from the deck. It's cold. But I'm hot.

And Dad's on the porch, I think, standing with Mum, which is nice because that never happens. Everyone's smiling. All those teeth.

But whatever, I keep going. Through the garden and there's the big gum tree with the brown bird box, except there's no birds in the tree or in the bird box. Why's that I wonder? But I keep going, over the lawn and across the dirt and I keep going past the brown shrubs and then it really is quiet I can't hear people talking or anything so I kind of feel a little alone. But that's nice too.

Down, down to the fence and there's the big skeleton trunk this big thing fallen over part of the fence and it's squashed it but no-one ever thought it needed fixing so it's always been there. Down, down the hill is the reserve and maybe I'll go there but I've forgotten the combination to the lock on the fence which is fine because we always used to just climb over the tree. So I grab it and hoist myself up and I climb up and as I do I cut my arm on a bit of barbed wire.

And it hurts.

It hurts like fuck.

It hurts…

like…

fuck!

And there's blood. There's red running down my arm, and there's a rip in my shirt.

And I'm thinking Dad will be pissed, 'Brand new shirt, Daniel!'

So I stand up on that old rotten tree trunk. And there's the ocean way in the distance. That blue ocean with the sun going down. And the city. There's the breeze. It's cold, but I'm hot. With blood running down my arm. Hurting like shit.

Hurting…

like…

> *Pause.*

And I cry. Just kind of burst. Not from the pain in my arm because I've had scratches like this before. Whatever. But I'm crying can't see the ocean or the city my eyes are stinging and it's hot standing on that tree.

Hot.

Standing on that tree crying. Standing there with the ocean and the city in front of me, heart going off in my chest.

> *DANIEL taps out a pacey rhythm across his chest.*

Therump therump therump. And I wish I… Because I didn't realise… that Bev would… that she was so… with those teeth.

Brown. Looking tired. Looking…
But people do. Don't they? People.
They die.
And I just hope. Just that. Well.
Bev knew. How I. What she.
You know?
I take a breath.
       Cold air.
My heart slows.

   DANIEL taps out a slowing rhythm across his chest.

Therump.
Ther
      ump.
           Ther
                  um um um
ump!
I turn back to the house.
Looks nice with the sun going down like that.

   A long pause.

I stand there for the longest time and then I…

For the longest time.

And then I head back up.

▼ ▼ ▼ ▼ ▼

SCRUB

GEORGIA GOODE

A GIRL, seventeen, stands in a bathtub.

The tap.
The water… it runs clear… it looks clean, but it's not.
It's not clean.
What comes out isn't clean.
It leaves this residue… a kind of scum around the edge.
When it dries it leaves this… stain. It's not mould or mildew or that shit that festers in the shower.
It's almost clear; kinda like a really fine powder.
The stain… it's getting harder and harder to scrub away.
He looks clean… I mean on weekends he doesn't shower and sometimes he doesn't shave his beard. Sometimes he sits on the couch and picks his toenails or does that thing with his saliva in the back of his throat. But… he looks clean; does that count? He looks like a good person. He wears a suit, he works and sleeps and dreams. He drinks coffee and rides a bike. He has a handsome face, I'm not sure if it's kind, but people say he's handsome.
The stains used to come off with natural products… baking soda, vinegar, eucalyptus oil.
Mum used to bang on about how we shouldn't use commercial cleaning products.
She said they were bad for us, that they're slowly poisoning the earth and infiltrating the water supply.
Arsenic is natural.
I read on the Internet that you can get arsenic poisoning from drinking water.
The water… looks clean but it isn't.
It attacks the organs of the body, the lungs, the skin, the kidneys, the liver. After a while you slip into a coma… and that's it, you're done for.

Scrub

Not everything that's natural is good for you.

I've done bad stuff before, like I've broken the rules, opened my mouth when I should've kept it shut. Kept it shut when I should have forced it open. But I'm mostly pretty clean.

One Christmas, years ago, Mum bought us ducklings. After they'd hatched and grown too big we put them in the bath. It must have been school holidays because we played with them for hours. I remember, when he went back to work at the bank... I was watching him shaving in the mirror. I was standing in the doorway, behind him. He was wearing a dark navy suit and shiny Italian shoes. The ducklings were in the tub, making a racket.

She laughs.

He just kept on shaving, softly chatting away to them while he went about his business... like it was the most normal thing in the world, to live in the middle of the city and have six ducklings in your bathtub.

He's dirty because he doesn't tell the truth. That's not what makes him dirty, it's that he lies... and doesn't feel any guilt. It's as if he breathes in clean air but what comes out is dirty. It's the kind of dirt that's hard to see, you have to get up really close to notice it. From a distance it just seems like he shimmers.

I'm dirty because sometimes I run in circles for a really long time and when you run in circles for a really long time you kick up all the dirt and it lands on other people.

We used to wash the dog in here, when we were kids. When the dog was still alive.

She hated it.

She laughs.

She would turn her head to face the wall as our little hands rubbed cheap shampoo into her coat.

He used to say, 'That dog, she's got some Irish in her, I tell you... she's so contrary'.

The shampoo left her smelling like lavender, which is a funny thing for a dog to smell like.

When we were done he would gently lift her from the bath. She was old by then.

When we'd drain away the water, there'd be fleas... stuck to the walls of the tub.

Sometimes they'd be stuck to him, trapped in the forest of his arm hair. We'd shriek and pull them off.

We loved that dog.

When I was small, I was certain that she was my mother. As though it were... just by accident that we happened to be of different species.

We were part of the same tribe. That dog and I.

Seems pretty stupid now. I mean... I look like my family, my parents. Weird that... isn't it? Like, some kind of genetic trick that happens when you're all related.

There is no dog now; no fleas either.

> *She turns on the tap and uses an old ice-cream container to swill water around the walls of the tub to rinse it clean.*

> *She sits on the wall of the tub facing the audience. We see her face.*

He's not sorry.

Do I have anything to be sorry for?

Maybe neither of us can ever be fully clean?

The lies... they've marked our skin; it's like there's all these little splinters just below the surface. I don't reckon we can pull them out.

The lies... they've made us bitter... made us close our eyes.

He opens his mouth.

Lie.

He reaches out to touch me.

Lie.

I smile.

Lie.

He's at work.

Lie.

I put my hands inside my pockets.

Scrub

Lie.
I laugh.
Lie.
I know.
He knows I know.
His nose is running.
True.
I'm late.
True.
He's not hearing me.
True.
He looks but doesn't see.
True.
He nods but doesn't understand.
True.
The water's dirty.
True.
The bathtub looks clean.
True.
But it isn't, it's stained.
And me? Am I?

▼ ▼ ▼ ▼ ▼

CHANGING ROOM

C.J. McLEAN

CHARLLEY, seventeen. A pre-op transgender person.
A small box of light in a sea of black. It's a changing room, made up of three walls (one of which has a peg on it) and a door. All the walls are mirrors, reflecting in on each other.
The door opens and CHARLLEY runs in, out of breath and clutching a bunch of 'boy clothes'. He is wearing baggy jeans, a t-shirt and hoodie, and a backpack.

Did she follow me? Can you tell?

> *He hangs the clothes up on the peg and pulls a checked shirt out of his bag. He holds it up to himself and looks at it in the mirrors.*

Yeah, it really works on me. I'm definitely having that.

> *He shows it to audience.*

What do you think?

> *He looks at the tag.*

A hundred dollars?! Who do they think they're kidding? Practically the same crap they're selling down at K-Mart. And their security's piss poor—it's usually just some thirteen-year-old on minimum wage who doesn't give two shits if you nick anything or not.
Like that kid they've got on the door. It's like he's barely there. He just stands there. What the fuck does he do all day? Shows how much money this place has got if they can pay someone to just *stand there.*
I came in, right, he took one look at me, and I could see the gears start up in his head. I could see him thinking, 'Looks like a boy… but I could be wrong.' I gave him a half-smile and a shrug, you know, like:

Changing Room

He mimes it.

Doesn't say anything. Just smiles.
I'm standing there going, 'Come on, mate, take a fucking stab at it. Fifty-fifty chance you'll get it right.'
I get it, he doesn't want to get it wrong.

Pause.

He takes off his hoodie and holds it up.

Hundred and fifty dollars, Myer. The jeans were a hundred and fifty dollars from David Jones and the t-shirt was seventy dollars from YD. The shoes were a fucking brilliant steal: they're genuine, Yeezy. I love them, 'cause there was this one guy who had his eye on me the whole time. Like, *the whole time.* I was in there for an hour and he only looked away for a second—but that was all I needed. I was gunning it quicker than anything.

He hangs the shirt up on the peg.

Just when he thought he'd got me I was gone. He was shouting and swearing—he was like, 'Catch that guy, he's fucking pinched, grab them!' But there was no way he was catching up to me. No way any of them were.
Sometimes I think it'd be fun to get caught, but they never can get me.
They think I'm an easy target, like I can't run fast or something. But then they try and chase after me. And they get it. I'm too good.
That's why I love doing it. Every kid, every dickhead with a name badge thinks when the moment comes, they'll chase them down, they'll catch the guy and be heroes. But most of the time they don't even notice! Stupid fat fucks. It's funny as hell.
The ones that do try, though, I love the look on their faces when they realise they've lost. It's great. I make sure I see it, as I'm running off. Just a quick turn, quick peek. They're out of breath, doubled over. But they're still going for it!

He laughs, a huge guffaw.

Fucking brilliant!
These guys—

He points at the changing room door.

If they knew how much I'd taken off them, they'd have a fucking heart attack.
I reckon they should just get better at their jobs! It's too easy sometimes. Started ages ago, when I saw these Vans I wanted. Pricey, but I was only thirteen then. I was angry. Am angry. And no-one was gonna notice.
I've been nicking shit for years and my parents haven't got wind of nothing, not teachers, not even the cops. I'm that good.

He starts to hold clothes up to himself, to see how they look. He stuffs a few in his bag that he likes.

I've been coming here for fucking ages and *they* don't know. Most of the time I'll even try stuff on before I take it. It's like a victory run, you know? Marking the territory. Like, 'I didn't just steal off you, I spent half an hour trying the goddamn clothes on!'
I like to look at myself in them. I love it…
I'm gonna look so fucking good when I've got that shirt.

There's a knock on the door.

Fuck off!

Pause.

I come in on Thursdays 'cause there's this girl that works here, every day, between two and five. I see her when I come in. And she's pretty noticeable—big lips, long hair, tight skirts…
And I know she sees me 'cause she'll always come over and ask if I need help. First thing she does. And she says… get this, she comes over and says, 'Do you need help finding anything, miss?'

Fuck that. I mean every time. Every. Time. So I say to her, 'I'm not a miss', and she starts apologising, goes, 'Oh my God, I'm so-o-o-o-o sorry, let me help you with that, sir'.

The first time I could've written it off as a mistake. But she kept doing it! I'd come in just to see if she'd try it again. I mean she did it just then! I walked in the store and *bam!* She was on me. I swear to God, she seeks me out! I was shitting myself, I thought she saw me put the shirt in my bag, so I started thinking of ways to get out of it and then…

She just said, 'Do you need help, miss?'

He takes off his t-shirt, revealing a bandaged chest, keeping down childlike breasts.

Like she'd come close to me if she didn't think she could fuck with me. She's *safe*, behind the counter, in her own skin. Her with her big lips and big hair and tight skirts… No-one will tell her she's done any harm. 'Cause she can afford to make mistakes, no-one's gonna bring her up on it, are they?

There's another knock.

I said, fuck off!

I think, like, in three months I'll be eighteen. Then I can have surgery. And if I came in here after that, just once, and she didn't say it, I'd be set. I'd be fucking set.

Would she know it was me?

No. She'd never know. She wouldn't stop to notice.

He mimics her.

'Can I help you, sir?'

'Yeah, I'm looking for something. I saw it in here a while ago, can you help me find it?'

'What were you looking for, sir?'

'Your phone number.'

He laughs, then stops himself.

Pause.

Smooth, Charlley.
What'd it be like to have her? Up against the wall, just fucking all night.
What if I were halfway through screwing her and then, and just as she's about to come, I lean down and whisper in her ear, 'Do you need help, *miss*?'
The look on her face. I'd give anything to see the look on her face.

He takes down the checked shirt and holds it against himself.

I love it.
And I'll get away with it.

Practising:

'I don't know how it ended up in my bag!'
'Okay, I took it, but I was gonna bring it back, seriously!'

He looks up. He sees something…

'So what if I stole it…'

It's a security camera, suspended over the box and looking in.

He immediately crouches down, shielding himself from the camera's gaze.

'… you owe me.'

He looks down at his bandages, then covers it with the shirt.

How long have you been there?

There's another knock on the door.

Is that you?

Knock.

Having a good laugh?
I get it. Okay? I get it!

Changing Room

He pulls stuff out of his bag, hangs it up.

There. I'll just leave them there, okay?

Knock.

Fuck off, alright?

Knock.

How long have you been fucking watching me?

Knock.

He jumps up, scales the walls, kicks, punches. Trapped.

Fuck off! Just fuck off, I'll be out in a minute just leave me alone, just leave me the fuck alone!

Knock.

You've got your shit back!
You've got my face. You've got this!

He points to his bandages.

What else do you want?

Knock.

You won't catch me!

Knock.

You can't see me!

Knock.

I can't come out yet. You can't see me like this.

He turns and sees himself in the mirror—heavy breathing, eyes wide, bandaged chest exposed.

I'm not ready.

Knock.

Knock.

Knock.

▼ ▼ ▼ ▼ ▼

THE FUZZ

KIRBY MEDWAY

JACOB walks into a costume shop and immediately becomes nervous when he notices Adam at the counter.

Hey, Adam. I didn't know you were working here. Did you just start or something? That's cool. I think it's great. It's great to have a job, great you have a job, I should probably get a job… [*with a nervous laugh*] … one of these days.

So, would it be okay if I spoke to your boss for a second? I know you're closing but I just wanted to return something and he said he was the only one who could do it. I know that seems a bit weird because you can probably do returns too but that's what he said and I guess we should honour his wishes here since it's his shop and everything and now he's your boss. So… if you could go get him…

Adam leaves and the boss emerges. JACOB looks around and then holds up a fake moustache.

So this was a dumb idea. That's not just directed at you either because I know it was my decision. How was this ever going to look like my own facial hair? And that's not meant to be an insult to your product; it's a fake, novelty moustache. If people believe it, it's not doing its job.

I was so close to going to the party last night too. I had it all figured out. I would show up, moustache on, and everyone would be like, 'Whoa, Jacob, nice moustache! When did you grow that? You look distinguished, like a police detective.' But I looked in the mirror one last time and realised how stupid all of this was. Plus, I wasn't all that invited to the party anyway.

I was feeling pretty hopeless, so I decided to go for a walk which, at first, wasn't such a great idea. It felt like everywhere I looked someone had a beard or some kind of facial hair and they were just walking around, enjoying themselves. Then I started to get that feeling again. Like this is just another thing I'm being left out of, except this time it's the forces of biology that are excluding me and it's not like I can do anything about that. But then I figured out what the real problem was. It's the transition. That's the key. No-one goes from clean-shaven to beard, and especially not to moustache, without someone noticing the process. If I want people to believe that I've grown facial hair they have to see the change. I have to go from clean-shaven to stubble then to beard and if we want to be really detailed there are probably even more stages in the beard phase.

So, I was hoping you could help me. I feel you kinda owe me a bit. That fake moustache thing was risky and nearly feels like you were setting me up for failure. This time we'll need your best stuff too. We might even need to custom-make the facial hair to get it just right. What do you think?

JACOB walks off and puts on fake stubble. He re-enters the store. It is now a week later. He is much more confident this time.

Hello, Adam! Glad you're keeping this job thing going, I bet it will look good on the old resume. I can tell you're playing what they call… 'the long game'. Very smart. I hope they're being good to you here. I'm just kidding, I'm sure they are, I'm sure they are. Anyway, I'm just here to speak to your boss… Derrick. Does he ever let you call him that? Doesn't matter. So, yeah. If you could go get him…

Adam leaves and the boss comes out. JACOB looks around and slowly removes his fake stubble.

Mr Harris… we're in. People are totally buying it. This is probably the best thing ever. I feel, I feel more mature. I feel like I can relate to people on a whole different level, a more even level. Someone actually called me 'sir' the other day. The best one though, when I was walking around at school I overheard another guy in my year saying, 'Hey, Jacob's finally getting some stubble'.

It's like I have become a totally different person. I'm much more comfortable and relaxed. Before the stubble, I sometimes didn't even know what to do with my hands. I would try keeping them by my sides or alternating between putting them in my side and back pockets. I even tried to pat someone on the back one time and it was just strange. I mistimed it, they got creeped out, it wasn't pretty. People even used to sing the words 'Puppet Hands' at me to the tune of 'Rocket Man'. But that's all behind me now. Last week, I actually did a complete high-five, including the down low part, without messing it up. It was awesome.

I really want to thank you for helping me with this. You could have just told me to stop whining and get over it, but the fact that you seem confident makes me think that this could really work. The thing that blows my mind is that this is just the beginning. I mean, a lot of guys in my school only have patchy and thin facial hair at best. What are people going to do when they see me walk in with a full beard? Which reminds me, I know the original plan was to leave it another week before starting the beard phase but I can't wait anymore. I think we have to do it now, while we've got some momentum. Are you ready?

JACOB exits and re-enters. More time has passed. He is clearly upset and is holding a fake beard in his hand.

Hey, Adam, can you get Dad to come out here?

Adam leaves and the boss comes out. JACOB holds up the beard.

Well, we didn't fool them. We never fooled them. Someone took me aside today and said that everyone knew pretty much the whole time. Apparently, the people who talked to me about my beard were just being ironic. They said that everyone else was just unsure what to say about it and that some were even a bit concerned. Then I pointed out, 'Why didn't the teachers say anything?', and they said, 'Didn't they?', which made me angry at first, but then I thought about it a bit. Mrs Cameron had said, 'That's going to get annoying', so I thought she was talking about when beards get itchy and food gets caught in them. And Mr Lansdowne asked me, 'When's that finally going to come off?' Which, at the time, seemed like he was asking about my shaving habits. Then there was that one substitute who said, 'Will you please take off that fake beard?', which I ignored so he just sighed and got on with things. I guess it was just wishful thinking.

How can I go back to the way things were now that I know how good it can be? Actually, because of all this, things probably won't just reset to how they were before anyway. I'll probably end up even lower on the social ladder, on whatever level there is for people who try to get taken more seriously… [*with a sigh*] by wearing fake beards. The worst part is that if I started growing facial hair tomorrow I bet no-one would even believe it was real.

Pause.

I'm sorry, you've been smirking pretty much the whole time I've been talking. I don't know if you've noticed but I'm having a bit of a hard time here and… Oh God.

Pause.

You think this whole thing is funny, don't you? Has this been a big joke to you the whole time? Oh, this is great… Yeah, I can hear you laughing back there, Adam. You guys suck, what kind of help is this? I bet you didn't even expect me to commit to this whole thing, did you? Well, guess what? I did. So who's the idiot now?

Pause.

Don't answer that. I guess it's my job to know when people are making fun of me.
Anyone looking for something genuine in a stupid costume shop is probably just asking for it anyway.
No, forget it. I've gotta go. I get it now anyway. We live in a cold world and I guess my face will just have to get used to the breeze.

JACOB storms out of the shop. He stops, shivers for a second and then walks off.

▼ ▼ ▼ ▼ ▼

NICE

GEMMA NEALL

LAURA, seventeen, bolts into a bathroom. She just makes it to the toilet before throwing up violently. Make-up is running down her face and her party clothes are crumpled and askew.
She wipes her eyes. The mascara smudges further.
She calls out to someone beyond the door.

I'm so sorry about this—I'm normally way more composed.
Did I throw up on you?

> *She groans*

I did, didn't I?
On your shoes?
That's so gross, I'm so sorry.

> *She stumbles away from the toilet and slumps against the bathroom door to talk to the person on the other side.*

You should really meet me when I'm sober. You'd love me when I'm sober. I'm a fucking delight.
My boyfriend normally looks after me when I'm like this, so thanks for being a stand-in.
Actually, fuck meeting me, you should meet Jeremy. He's my boyfriend. He's such a sweetheart.
It was my birthday last week, right? And he got me this teddy—you know one of those where you can record your voice and like:

> *She mimics the bear.*

'I wuv you, Laura.'
'You are so b-e-a-utiful.'
It was the cutest thing ever you would have died.

LAURA lurches forward and vomits into the toilet again. She grips onto the porcelain bowl as an anchor.

That was the first thing he ever said to me.
See, we met at the bus stop in front of my school.
I was being sent home early after I grazed my face on the bitumen in PE and he tells me that I look beautiful.
No-one had ever said that to me before.
I'm sitting there crying, face full of snot and pebbles probably still lodged in there, and he tells me that I'm the most beautiful thing he's ever seen.
I mean, can you believe it?
All these people in the world and I'm beautiful?
I felt so lucky.
What a fucking dream, right?
And Dad loves him.
So there's that.

She throws up again and wipes her mouth on the back of her hand.

Sorry.
He's just really lovely.
You'd love him, I swear.
That sounds bad, does that sound bad?
I don't mean it to be.
Honest.
He's so nice.
Like, when he couldn't come to the formal with me, he bought me a corsage and danced with me in his living room.
It was almost as good as being there.

Pause.

His friends are a pack of wankers though.
No, well, that's not fair. Not really. They're boys and boys can be dicks sometimes I guess, but I always thought that when you were older you grew out of that.

God, not that they're *old* old or anything.

They call me 'Jailbait' and I'd probably be more annoyed by that if Jeremy didn't just hold me close and tell me he loves me. I'm *his* girl.

She puts her head in her hands and groans.

I don't feel good.

I only really came in here because Shane—you know Shane, from English?—well, anyway, Shane won't leave me the fuck alone.

I had to run in here just to get away from him.

She glances at the toilet bowl where she's been throwing up.

Lucky thing I did, I guess.

Not so lucky for your shoes though.

Sorry.

Shane did that thing before—you know when you're just standing there and they're like, 'What, don't I get a hug?' Like, no, fuck off. I don't know you.

But I didn't want to look like a bitch so…

I hate that.

Pause.

Jeremy asked for a hug that first day as I was getting onto the bus. He'd just put his number into my phone.

But that's different.

I wanted it.

Shane's a dick.

Jeremy picks me up from school every day. He used to wait right out front, but someone must have said something to him because now he waits around the corner.

But he's there every day.

It's nice.

Really.

LAURA stumbles to her feet and begins fixing her make-up in the mirror.

D'you reckon Shane's gone now?
Maybe I should have chundered all over him instead.
Sorry again.
I do feel kind of bad for him I guess.
Jeremy says I shouldn't be surprised if people like me.
He says that I'm special.
Though no-one really did before him.
He's made me better.
He sees me, you know?
He looks after me.
That's good, isn't it?
Dad thinks so.
Dad met him and it was like a fucking job interview. I was so embarrassed.
It was all:

Mimicking her father:

'Take care of her',
and shit like that.
I'm not a child.
If it were an interview, Jeremy was exactly the kind of candidate Dad was looking for.
He loves me.
So that's good.
Right?
He loves me and he wants to show me he loves me.
It's fine. Good.
It's nice to be wanted, and Jeremy wants me.
The sex only hurt a little after the first time.
I read that happens though.
So that's okay.
It's good.
And when I said that I didn't want to do it anymore because I wasn't ready, Jeremy was really good about it.
He even cried, he'd felt so bad about stuffing up like that.

We still sleep together.
But it's nice.
Really.

Pause.

Mum's a bit funny around him though.
If she's home when Jeremy's over she doesn't really like to
leave us alone.
But like, she had me pretty young though, so I guess I get it.
We spend most of our time at his anyway.

*LAURA jumps, reacting to the buzzing of a phone in her
pocket. She pulls it out to look at the text message.*

It's Jeremy.
We text a lot when we're not together.
He likes to know where I am and who I'm with.
What we're doing.
It's sweet.
He worries about me.

She types out a reply to the text.

If I don't message back he'll start calling.
Only because he wants to be sure that I'm okay.
He'll pick me up soon.
I'm only supposed to be here for a few hours. He doesn't like to
leave me alone for long.
He's nice.
Really.
I'm talking too much again, aren't I?
I always do,
Dad says boys would like me better if I kept quiet.
But Jeremy likes me anyway.
He says he doesn't mind, but then his eyes glaze over and I
feel like he might be lying.

She begins to straighten her party clothes.

Jeremy bought this outfit for me.
I feel…
felt…
feel so lucky when he looks at me.

Pause.

Mum thinks I should see a counsellor.
We celebrated his birthday just the two of us at this Indian restaurant near his house. Everyone sang as they brought out the cake.
It had twenty-nine candles.

She moves to sit on the edge of the bathtub.

Sometimes I find it hard to be near him.
I don't mean that in a bad way or anything, he's just intense.
Like you'll burn if you get too close.
I'm his girlfriend. His *girl*. I've never been anyone's anything before.
Is girlfriend even the right word?
I'm probably just not used to it.
Do you think you can make yourself love a person?
Not that I don't.
I mean…
he's so nice.

A knock on the door.

LAURA jumps. She's forgotten where she was.

She calls out to the person outside.

I'll come out soon.
Really.
I just need a rest.

A buzz. Another text. She types a quick reply.

He'll be thirty next year.

Nice

Is it weird no-one his own age will date him?

Pause.

I didn't mean that.

She stands and straightens her clothes, preparing to leave.

Mum wants me to run.
Dad thinks I should marry him.

The phone in her hand begins to vibrate with a call. She frowns at the screen.

▼ ▼ ▼ ▼ ▼

RED BULL

RACHEL O'REGAN

Note: This monologue is intended to get faster and faster as it is being performed, as if mimicking the effects of caffeine.
LEE is sitting in the exam room, staring at her paper, chewing through a pencil.

Question Three. Essay. An individual's identity is shaped by the way they perceive their connections with others and the world around them. How is this view represented in the prescribed text…

… Oh, my God. I can smell it. I can actually smell it on her breath. And I'm not surprised. Gabby drank four Red Bulls today, one after the other. Four. And not, like, the mini cans either. The new big cans with 'thirty-five per cent extra value'. I've read the warning labels, you can't drink more than one of those in a day. It's actually going to kill her. Her heart's going to explode. Oh, shit, I hope she's not going to die in here. That would really suck.

She twirls her pencil around.

They say a girl from a selective killed herself in an exam. Just stood up during four-unit maths and held two HB pencils to her nostrils and smashed her head down on the desk. *Bam!* The pencils went straight into her brain and killed her. Though, to be fair, she was doing four-unit maths so she was kind of asking for it.

Oh, shit. I can actually smell Red Bull coming out of her pores.

She shoots her hand up.

Miss? Can I be moved? Can I be moved? I can't concentrate, can I sit on my own? Please?

She slumps forward.

It's a competition, I've figured it out—who can freak out in the most melodramatic way possible. You know Tim's going for gold, taking his little sister's Ritalin. Says it helps him 'focus'. I've never seen *anyone* lose weight that quickly before. Zaid is drinking during the daytime, I think we've all watched enough 'Neighbours' to know how that turns out. And Kate— she won't take off her jumper. It's *October*. Everyone knows she's cutting herself again.

She pauses, rattled by her own hardness. She puts her head down and reads the paper again.

An individual's identity is shaped by the way they perceive their connections with others and the world around them…
Okay, an individual's identity…
An individual's identity…
It's this piece of paper.
It's multiple answer bubbles, short responses, essays. It's bands, ranks, practice papers, assessments, weighting, bell curves, bonus marks, trials, ATAR, UAC, standard, advanced, visual reps, Shakespeare, Skrzynecki, belonging, two-unit, four-unit, majors, estimates, extensions, *fucking scaling*. And for what?
I had a dream last night about the world ending. I mean, really ending. Fire raining from a blood sky, rivers of sulphur bubbling up, meteors crashing to the earth, the whole Board of Studies getting fucked in the arse by Satan's pitchfork, and in the middle of all of this death and destruction there's Gabby with her can of Red Bull and her goddamn study group, saying, 'I wonder if I'll get special consideration for this'.
You know, the worst part is, she's acting like she's totally fine. Like it's 'Just to stay awake', and she 'Won't need it after exams are over'. Like she hasn't been drinking at least two cans of Red Bull a day for the last five months. I've watched her gulp them down, one after the other, highlighting, underlining and rewriting those damn study notes she bought from the Band Six black market. And I told her, 'Gab, this isn't normal. Remember when you used to be my best friend, not looking over my shoulder to see what mark I got?' And Gabby just looked at me, this look that cut through me like ice, like I'm the one who needs help. 'Lee. Some of us actually have to study'.

An individual's identity is shaped…
Everyone thinks I'll ace this, don't they? They all think I'm
going to get ninety-nine, become a doctor or a lawyer. They
don't know how much they've been tricked. I should hand it
to myself, I've always known how to just get by, some people
would call it a talent except it's not. Scratch under the surface,
and it's all Wikipedia and thesaurus and tutors. It's not enough.
Not out here in the real world.
An individual's identity is shaped…
I don't know what happened. I knew what I had to do all along,
my God, I'd planned out every day… But every time I sat down
to study I was… I don't know, paralysed. I looked at my books
and my practice essays and I couldn't, I just couldn't… breathe.
I just went and watched TV to make the feeling go away, but
when I came back the feeling was worse because I'd wasted
even more time. So I went away and watched TV again, or got
something to eat, or wandered the house talking to the dog.
I kept telling myself, I promise, I will do this later, I just have
to give myself a rest first, and then it was lunch, dinnertime,
suddenly, four in the morning, the day before exams, freaking
out and my heart is beating out of my chest like I've drunk a
hundred Red Bulls because I've done nothing and—

The teacher sounds off, 'One minute to go'.

Shit. Oh, shit, shit. Quick. An individual's identity is shaped
by… Fuck!

*She desperately starts scribbling something down but it's
too late.*

What have you done? Shit, you lazy, useless, pathetic, self-
pitying, weak, stupid, stupid brainless piece of shit, loser, God,
you idiot, idiot, fucking idiot.
An individual's identity…

*A bell sounds. We hear the teacher call for pencils down. LEE
grabs two pencils and looks at the audience. She rears her
head back and the lights go down as we hear a loud crack.*

▼ ▼ ▼ ▼ ▼

POSSESSION

MORGAN ST. CLAIR

Lights up.
JONTY, a seventeen-year-old boy, sits at a plastic, tacky
restaurant table. He is nervous, but retains some confidence.

Okay, here we go.
Ask her something—
About herself, that's what they like, right?
They like talking about themselves…
Oh God, look at her…
No no no, not like that, you creep!
Eyes up, boy, eyes up.

Hmmm… Okay, so you seen anything good on the telly lately?
Or maybe…
Movies…?
Hey, I know, what's your favourite subject at school?

   He groans.

God, Jonty, what are you, her fucking Italian textbook? *Io*
preferito… Shit!
—

Yeah, bet you can't wait till school's over, hey? All those
exams… I mean, I like some of them… You know, I used to like
Ancient History? Reckon those Persian wars were pretty cool.
You know, Spartan phalanxes and shit…
—

Na na, I swear, mate, they're actually like the coolest…
Fine, fine, haha… Guess you can stick to your fucking…
What was it again? French, French of course… O la la…
—

Speaking of French…

I wonder if her parents are home…
I wonder if *my* parents are home, if I could…
—

Yeah, I love this place, doesn't look like much, but the steaks are incredible.
Top proper meat.
—

Oh, really?
I'm… I'm sorry…
I thought…
I really thought you'd like it.
I mean not just the food but look at that view…
—

He looks at her.

Look at that smile.
—

Sorry, can I just interrupt you there to tell you you've got a lovely smile?
—

Anyway, what were you saying about…?
—

Oh, I mean… but we've already ordered and everything…
—

No no… if you really don't like it…
Hey hey, I know, how about, how about, once the food arrives we get it takeaway, right, and we go sit down on that, bench, down there, on the beach?
—

Yeah?
Okay, cool. Well, sorry about that… I guess…
I didn't really…

He sighs and looks around, before noticing someone in the corner.

Watch it, you in the corner, I can see ya, mate, keep your eyes
down, that ain't yours to ogle at.
Ya dick.
She's mine.
Well, I mean…
Not exactly *mine*, not mine exactly.
But she's here with me, alright?

Yeah here,
with little old me,
girl like her…
Fuckin' hell.

Anyway,

    He shakes himself.

what do you want to study at uni?

—

Women's Studies? That's a thi—

—

Oh, of course it's a thing of course, of course, but like, what
can you do with that?

—

Wow right. That's crazy. Don't you reckon though that there
could be other shit you could be doing too? I mean—

    He jumps.

—

Okay okay, I'm sorry I'm sorry, I get it, but I just don't really
think that, like, that's the biggest problem? I mean, don't little
kiddies in Africa still—

—

But we ain't there yet, are we? And are we ever… I mean,
you're not going to invite me back to your house tonight,
later…
alone…

A stranger sort of,
are you?

—

Would she?

—

No of course not, 'cause you're a clever chick and you know
there are rapists in the world.
Not saying I was going to rape you or anything, ha ha.
Just…
Erm…
I guess I'm trying to say that…
There's got to be more to it than that, right?

—

Yeah, go on.

—

Man-spread— ?

> *He looks down and notices his legs splayed open. He*
> *straightens himself and brings his knees together.*

Right. Fuck, I've never noticed that.

—

I didn't realise girls felt like that. I suppose it's the same with
where guys look too hey, I mean with the—

> *He gestures to the chest area.*

But I mean where am I meant to look? They are practically
spilling out of her top! If I look her in the eyes she's going to
think I'm too intense or like deliberately not looking but still
thinking about them and wanting to look which is kinda true
and if I look at her nose she'll think I'm not paying attention
and if I look down I'm just looking at them— okay okay, maybe
just kinda hover between her lips and her eyes…

Yeah, that's kinda sexy, isn't it?
Makes her think I'm going to kiss her…

Oh God, am I going to kiss her?

Possession

No no no, not now, not yet anyway. Later on, maybe.

Shit, do I get the bill or does she?
No, you get the bill that's what a gentleman does…
Like Don fucking Draper, mate.

But I guess the fifties and sixties were pretty sexist, right? All that 'in the kitchen' stuff…
So… half and half? That's equal. Fair?
Nah, 'cause then that's just like we're fucking married already, right, like boy's gotta do something to impress her…

And maybe if I get it I'll get…

Maybe we'll just play that one by ear…
—

Umm, well,
I work on Dad's farm.
Got my own cattle actually—yeah, dropped out last year, soon as I could, y'know, family business and legacy and all that.

I have actually been thinking about going back, maybe, and finishing up?
Doing something at TAFE later in agriculture…

Um, so, what do you do for work, Blythe?
—

He chokes in surprise.

What?
—

Sorry, no I don't.
I'm just…
surprised.
Well, I just thought you'd have to be over eighteen?
—

Yeah, course. Wow.

He stops and realises.

Bet her foreplay is Olympic, mate.

He gives himself a self-high five

—

But do you...
Do you like it?
But...
But isn't that kind of fucking gross?
Hearing it all?
Doesn't that just make...

—

I guess... yeah, I guess I can see... I mean, how much money we talking here?

—

He chokes again in surprise.

—

What?!
Are you fucking serious?
Guess that fucking settles the bill conundrum then.
Wow. Mate, can I have a job? Ha ha, just kidding, not actually, I would never—
No no no,
Of course you—
I mean I'm different, I mean sorry, I'm not *different*, I'm not like, better than you or anything but like, but you know...
I'm a guy so...
Why would I?

—

What? No sorry I'm...
I can't stop picturing...
It's different she only...

But all those—

With their...

Possession

Words in her ear…

Oh…

—

No, sorry, I'm not saying you should be ashamed or anything.
I guess you must have pretty thick skin by now, ay?
You'd have to, I reckon.
To put up with that.
It's impressive, I guess?

That you keep on.

—

You know, it'd be okay.
If you wanted to, to keep on…
If we…
I mean, I'm all for it, taking back, the power of it, getting paid,
all that jazz, but girl, that's heavy—
Wait,
You…
You weren't going to tell me, were you?

—

Fuck.

—

Well… I have a right to know?! Why? Why because I'm on a
fucking date with you and what if—
Well, what if…
I wanted you to be my girlfriend?
Well, not right now, I mean…
it's way too soon to be talking like that.
I'm just saying…
In the future…
I mean, we don't know…
Like, you're super hot and…
funny…
and you're way more clever than me.
So I guess you're out of my—

But like, I don't care about that stuff—well I do,
You know I kinda would?
If you were… if you were my girl…

I wouldn't want all those nasty fat—

panting in your ear.

I can see them.

It's disgusting.

How…

could you…

you're…

Come on, here's our food.

Let's get out of here.

I want to…

take you somewhere.

▼ ▼ ▼ ▼ ▼

BRIGHT

CIELLA WILLIAMS

The feeling.
When it—
When it's not
Yours anymore

A house
His house
A bed
Not his
Doesn't matter

He comes in
Into my room
I'm not worried.
He's my friend.
I kind of like that he came in
That he wants—
I'm glowing redskin vodka pink, lights spinning under my lids.
But I don't—

There's a look.

Mum loves us so much.
Mum dresses me up and shows me off.
— My babies!
— My clever boy.
— My beautiful girl.
— Isn't she beautiful?
I want to be. Beautiful. Like her.
She is golden.
When I put my face to her skin I feel it.

Hot, on my cheek.
She brushes my hair. She ties up my dress.
And she opens up my chest—and screws in the bulb.
—Beautiful girl.
Bing!

I'm Poison Ivy. Felix is Mr Freeze.
My room is our base.
I know how to do it. How to copy the hippety hips and fluttery lashes.
I wear my bathers because they kind of look like Poison Ivy's suit.
All girl supervillains look like this. It's their power.
—And and and I use my potion and Batman falls in love with me—
—Yeah and then I have a ray gun—
—And then you go—
—and then and then and then—
Felix says I should put socks in my top to look more like her.
I shove two pairs of Dad's work socks down my front.
One
Two
Mash them into shape.
Tadah!
And Felix looks at me—in a way—in a new way
and I
start to glow.

   She is strutting around the room.

Girls are sexy, made out of Pepsi, boys are rotten, made out of cotton.

I've got a new beanie baby.
He's a boy. Jemima's is a girl.
They're going out.
And they—

Beat.

—Does it make you feel…?
—Yeah.
—Where?
—There.
—Yeah. Same.
—Warm.
—Yeah. Like that.

Steph tells me to
Jump
It'll make your boobs grow.
Like this. Jump. Like, little ones.
Bounce
I close my eyes
Imagine I'm getting brighter.
The wooden floor is bouncing with us.
—*What are you girls doing up there?*
We're gonna be seen.

—Jess got hot!
—I just grew some boobs. Dickhead.
Roll my eyes.
But
I'm glowing.
He can probably see. Probably I want him to see.
There's a little hippety hip in my walk.
Girls are sexy, made out of…

Fire, my face is burning, and I am free-dom, and I am bass
boom booming in my blood and I am the best fucking dancer
in the *whole world* and I am tiny, tiny, tiny, so, so tiny, and I am
huge, I am exploding light, so bright, like a nuclear bomb and
no-one can look away, and I'm my own PJ Harvey song, I'm in
a French film, I'm my whole future and I can do anything, go
anywhere, I'm so fucking bright, even if they want to touch
me, they know they can't 'cause they'll get burnt.

Mum looks at me
Like she hates it
Like it hurts her eyes
Like she can't remember that
It's hers
She put it there.
I know
I know she would switch me off
If she could.

He likes my light.
Sees it
Brighter than the bonfire the headlights the moon.
We walk away
From the smoke and the crunching speakers and the bodies in the sand.
We walk close enough that he's lit up by me
Globe burning hot
Close enough that I'm in his haze
Spray deodorant
And sugar bourbon breath.
I'm scared we might ignite
And I think I hope we do
The sand dunes smell of wet ash and salty bottles. And... new smells.
You
Me
This
We
This
Shake. From the adrenaline. My heart is beating here, here [*head*], here, here [*neck*], here, here [*stomach*], and I don't know if I liked it
But it was mine.
And I can see that he
He liked it.

Bright

And I'm charged.

My room
My bed
Making shadows on the ceiling
A heart.
A bird.
Fingers weaving
Knitting
Hiding the light
And letting it out.

The band is so loud
I don't hear it
I feel it
Behind my eyes
In my chest
Glass buzzing
The bodies are big
and slick
and crushing.
It smells like men and booze and mud
And I'm soaked in all of it
I feel eyes on me
I'm lighting them up
The waves are hurtling through the crowd
I'm bouncing off hips and ribs
I like the skin
I like the weight
I'm pushing *back*
Pressing into the ones I like
The arms
The chests
The crotches
There's a thousand glowing hands above the black sea
Everyone is reaching

Some guy
His hands are on my hips
I'm going up
I'm pressing my thighs
My—
Into the heat of his neck.
Bouncing
Denim riding
Sweat mixing
My light's streaming out my mouth
I'm a spotlight
Pointing straight up
Beaming.

A house
His house
A bed
Not his
I'm glowing redskin vodka pink
I kind of like that he came in
That he wants—
But I don't—
Lights spinning under my lids.

He's in the bed.

I roll over.
Away.
His hands move under my t-shirt
The silence is
so
loud.
I feel it.
I say
I don't
I don't
Under my lids. White and blue. Burning.

Bright

His hands
Touch the skin on my back

And

The light.

He's taken it.

It's in his fingers

I can feel them

Red
hot.

Setting fire to the nerves on my back.

A room
A house
Not mine
Doesn't matter

My heart beating [*head*] here, here, [*neck*] here, here, [*chest*]
here, here.

Dark

But the bulb—
I'd feel the glass
Rattle
In my chest
If it was broken.
I don't
I feel—

▼ ▼ ▼ ▼ ▼

AUTHOR BIOGRAPHIES

YARRIE BANGURA *(A Long Walk Home)*

Yarrie Bangura is a writer, performer, musician, visual artist, textile designer and public speaker. She most recently was a performer and writer in *The Baulkham Hills African Ladies Troupe* which was presented at Belvoir and Riverside in 2013; and in 2015 at the Southbank Centre, London; Nottingham Playhouse, UK; Sydney Opera House; and had a return season at Riverside Theatres. Yarrie has also performed in *Frolic* (BigWest Festival, Melbourne), *Slaves* (African Theatre Troup/BYDS) and *Nga Woray—My Mother's Wooden Spoon* (Shopfront). Yarrie is one half of the band Sierra Sisters whose music has been featured on several commercials and Triple J Unearthed. She has been a member of the Sierra Leone Cultural Performance Dance Group since 2006, performing at events around Sydney. Yarrie writes poetry, short stories, autobiographical work and plays. She is currently a Special Youth Representative for Australia for UNHCR.

MICHAEL J. CORNFORD *(Lazlo's Feet)*

Only a cub scout at the time, Michael Cornford was made to do drama classes as a child after proclaiming a desire to be a comedian. Instead, he spent seven years learning to be a tree and, during his HSC, teaching others to be a tree at the Central Coast's Mad Cow Theatre Company. Michael went on to study a Bachelor of Media and Communications at the University of New England, in Armidale, but in reality spent all his time in the theatre department. Here, he developed a love of dramatic writing, primarily in the form of adaptation at that time. While still performing, he made opportunities for himself to direct performances and step on toes to make things happen. Buchner's *Woyzeck*, Pinter's *The Dumb Waiter* and Bovell's *Speaking in Tongues* are some of his proudest directing achievements.

Upon leaving Armidale, Michael applied successfully to study at NIDA in the Technical Theatre and Stage Management degree. He believes that technical problem-solving and stagecraft are some of the most important things to get work on its feet. While at

Biographies

NIDA Michael has worked on numerous projects and productions. A highlight was Michael Gow's production of *Writing for Performance—A Personal View*. In what spare time Michael has found while at NIDA, he has written a full-length play, *Burden on Society*, along with numerous shorter works, including *Love Me Do* (a short play) which had its first production in 2015, and *Speak Some Speech* (a short film) currently in development.

ALBERTO DI TROIA *(Coast)*

Alberto Di Troia is an emerging Melbourne-based writer/director and a graduate of the Bachelor of Film and Television at the Victorian College of the Arts. Before being accepted into the degree, Alberto's play *Queenie Beth* won honours at the South Australian State Theatre Young Playwrights Awards. For the 2011 Adelaide Fringe, Alberto wrote, directed and produced his play *The Housesitters* to a sold-out season and critical success. His graduating short film *Blood Trust* was awarded Best Undergraduate Screenplay by the VCA and has played at festivals both nationally and internationally. He is also the recipient of the VCA Film & TV Department's Lionel Gell Foundation Scholarship and Erwin Rado Memorial Prize for Excellence. Alberto is currently working on long-form film and theatre projects and recently worked as an assistant editor on the upcoming Australian feature film *Downriver*.

PIRI EDDY *(Teeth)*

Piri Eddy is a writer, musician and stand-up comic. He has reviewed for *Heckler*, *Transnational Literature*, and London-based publication *The Upcoming*. He has also produced work for *Adelaide Indaily*, *Southern Write Magazine* and *Empire Times*. His photography and unsubstantiated insights into life and travel are all infrequently featured on his blog: thejourneysnowhere. wordpress.com. Piri's writing credits for theatre and performance include *Tonight With Tony* (2011, Neverender Productions), *Amuse Bouche* (2012, Neverender Productions) and *Comedy Action Rangers* (2013, The Loose Five Productions). As a stand-up comedian, he has performed alongside some of Australia's finest comics, including Fiona O'Loughlin and Peter Berner. In 2013 Piri was a writer-in-residence at the SA Writers' Centre. 2015 saw him commence his PhD in Creative Writing at Flinders University, as well as being a participant in atyp's Fresh Ink national mentoring program.

GEORGIA GOODE (Scrub)

Georgia Goode is one of the many twenty-something-year-olds still figuring out what she wants to be. She attended atyp as a teenager and later went on to study acting at the Guildhall School of Music and Drama, London, and Screen Acting at the London Academy of Music and Dramatic Art. She is now interested in trying her hand at the other end of the creative process. Georgia grew up in and around the theatre in NSW as her parents believed it to be cheaper than paying a babysitter (cheers guys!), and this inspired her love of playwriting. She holds a Bachelor of Communication and Journalism from the University of New South Wales. As a journalist, Georgia has enjoyed writing other people's stories; however, she has recently taken up creative writing in order to tell a few of her own. Georgia currently works at Belvoir St Theatre in Sydney and owns two dogs named Rufus and Frankie.

C.J. McLEAN (Changing Room)

Callum 'C.J.' McLean is a playwright and review writer based in Adelaide. His creative work has appeared in InDaily, and was twice broadcast on Coast FM. He has written reviews for Buzzcuts (a part of Express Media) and Empire Times. He received two commendations for his script work in the South Australian State Theatre Company's Young Playwrights Award competition: in 2010 for Call Me Lolita, and 2013 for The Pink Elephant. He travelled to Guangzhou, China, as part of the AsiaBound project in 2015 to mentor Creative Writing students at Sun Yat-sen University's South and Zhuhai campuses. In 2014, he attended Oxford University's Creative Writing summer school, and studied with playwright Shaun McCarthy. He is part of the planning and editing committee for Flinders University's public speaking event Speakeasy, and their associated zine. He is currently completing his Honours in Creative Arts (Creative Writing) at Flinders University.

Biographies

KIRBY MEDWAY *(The Fuzz)*

Kirby Medway is a Sydney-based writer and performer as well as an occasional sound designer and composer. Some of his most recent contributions include the sound design for *As I Lay Dreaming* which was performed at Shopfront in 2015. He wrote *Encounter* which was first performed at the Woodcourt Art Theatre in 2013 before being presented at the Adelaide Fringe Festival in 2014. He spent most of 2013 touring around Australia performing poetry-themed shows to high school students with the theatre-in-education company Poetry in Action. Later that year, he wrote the text for *Ragnarök/or how it ended/*, which was presented as part of 'Civic Life' at Shopfront. He also composed the music for *The Defence* which has since toured to Melbourne and Western Australia. As a devisor and performer, he has presented work at a number of festivals such as the Festival of Dangerous Ideas, Under the Radar, Underbelly Arts and the Crack Theatre Festival.

GEMMA NEALL *(Nice)*

Gemma Neall is a former member of the Senior Ensemble of the now sadly defunct Urban Myth Youth Theatre Company. She studied a Bachelor of Arts in Creative Writing at Flinders University, and attended a Creative Writing Summer School at Oxford University in the summer of 2013. She trained as a dancer before developing a passion for theatre and moving into acting. Recent credits include *Origin of the Species* and *Romeo and Juliet*, both with Urban Myth. She enjoys working with young people to create theatre and is currently writing a play about the Australian war heroine Nancy Wake. She lives in Adelaide with her pet succulent Fergus.

RACHEL O'REGAN *(Red Bull)*

Rachel O'Regan has always been excited by two things: writing and acting. While she wasn't so good at the latter, she now writes professionally for *I Quit Sugar* and *fangirls* over amazing acting performances in the privacy of her own home (and blog). She now wants to bring the two obsessions together with playwriting. She is currently developing her first full-length play, *FULL*, a 'realistically twisted' tragicomedy about disordered eating and disordered families.

MORGAN ST. CLAIR *(Possession)*

Morgan St. Clair is a writer, dancer and painter based in Sydney, NSW. Her acceptance into Newtown High School of the Performing Arts (NHSPA) for her HSC years saved Morgan from the depths of suburbia and the prison-yard politics of an all-girls school in Sydney's west. Those years at NHSPA opened Morgan up to the idea that being a 'creative' is a multifaceted, complex experiment that takes years to come to any sort of coherent form. Morgan then spent her first couple of years out of school travelling around Europe, surviving South America and living in London for a year. During her travels Morgan was drawn more and more to writing. It is something that she has always done, instinctively, yet it was only in those years that she started to seriously consider it as something she wanted to do all the time, full-time and forever. Now studying a Bachelor of Communications, majoring in Creative Writing, at UTS, Morgan, after some life-changing plays given to her by her high achieving theatre-making friends, and after some late-night stream of consciousness experiments with playwriting, feels like she has finally touched on something that rings true with her. She is thrilled and excited to explore this and where it will take her.

CIELLA WILLIAMS *(Bright)*

Ciella Williams is a Darwin-born actor and theatre-maker, and is starting to venture into writing. She studied at Melbourne University but loves living and creating work in the Northern Territory. Ciella recently developed a satirical cabaret show called *The Sicko Glitter Sisters Present: The True Blue Straight and Narrow Normal People's Club* with C.J. Fraser-Bell. The two collaborated in 2014 to develop *Frankensteined Monologues* as the Theatre of the Found Collective, and presented it at the Crack Theatre Festival in Newcastle. In 2015, Ciella performed in the development of *Coal Face* by Sarah Hope, and in *Broken* by Mary Anne Butler as part of Brown's Mart Theatre's Shimmer Season. Ciella is a core working member of the Darwin Fringe Festival Committee, and is involved with a group of young artists committed to making new work and new performance opportunities in Darwin.

▼ ▼ ▼ ▼ ▼

MENTOR BIOGRAPHIES

LACHLAN PHILPOTT is a Sydney-based writer and teacher.

As a playwright he has worked with The American Conservatory Theatre San Francisco, Amnesty International, Australian Theatre for Young People, Belvoir Sydney, Bell Shakespeare, Brisbane Powerhouse, Canberra Youth Theatre, Checkpoint Theatre Singapore, Cre8ion, Crowded Fire Theater San Francisco, Edinburgh Festival, Feast Festival Adelaide, Focus Theatre Sydney, Glen St Theatre Sydney, Griffin Theatre Company Sydney, Hothouse Theatre Albury, IronBark London, Kansas State University, La Boite Brisbane, The Lark New York, London Pride, Magic Theatre San Francisco, Mardi Gras Sydney, The Mac Belfast, Midsumma Melbourne, Melbourne Festival, MKA New Writing Theatre, The New Theatre, NIDA, Outburst Belfast, Oval House London, Perth Theatre Company, Playwriting Australia, Q Theatre Penrith, PACT Sydney, The Perseverance Juneau, The NSW Drama Ensembles, The Playwrights' Center Minneapolis, The Playwrights Foundation San Francisco, Rock Surfers Sydney, Sydney Theatre Company, TheatreofplucK Belfast, The Traverse Theatre Edinburgh, Tantrum Theatre Newcastle, Red Stitch Melbourne, St Martins Melbourne, The Victorian College of the Arts and The Victorian Arts Centre.

Lachlan's plays include *Bison*, *Bustown*, *Catapult*, *Colder* (winner R.E. Ross Trust Award), *Lake Disappointment*, *M.ROCK*, *Silent Disco* (winner Griffin Award for Outstanding New Australian Play, winner GAP Competition Aurora Theatre Co. USA, winner Best Stage Play, Australian Writers' Guild Awards), *The Chosen*, *Truck Stop* (winner Best Play, Young Audiences Australian Writers' Guild Awards) and *The Trouble with Harry*. He has had nine plays published.

Lachlan has also done extensive work as a teacher, mentor and dramaturg at theatre companies, schools and tertiary institutions around the world. As the inaugural Australian Professional Playwright Fulbright Scholar, Lachlan was playwright-in-residence at The American Conservatory Theatre San Francisco in 2014/2015. Lachlan is Chair of the Australian Writers' Guild Playwrights Committee.

TOM HOLLOWAY is an award-winning playwright based in Melbourne, Australia.

His work has been seen across Australia, as well as in the UK, Europe and the Middle East. His credits in Australia include *Storm Boy* for Sydney Theatre Company and Barking Gecko, *Forget Me Not* and *Love Me Tender* for Belvoir, and *And No More Shall We Part* and *Don't Say the Words* for Griffin. His United Kingdom productions include *And No More Shall We Part*, produced by Hampstead Theatre and Traverse Theatre for the 2012 Edinburgh Fringe, and *Fatherland*, produced by The Gate Theatre and ATC. His play *Forget Me Not* will be produced by The Bush Theatre this December, and he has been the librettist on the opera *South Pole*, premiering at Bavarian State Opera in Munich in January 2016. Tom is currently under commission with Manhattan Theatre Club and Melbourne Theatre Company.

NICKI BLOOM's debut play *Tender* was first produced by nowyesnow in May 2007 as part of the B-Sharp downstairs season at Company B Belvoir in Sydney. This production then toured to Hothouse Theatre (Albury) and Griffin Theatre Company (Sydney), playing as part of the mainstage subscription seasons at both theatre companies. In July 2009 *Tender* was produced by the Summer Play Festival at the Public Theater's Anspacher space in New York City, USA. *Tender* also received a reading at London's Donmar Warehouse in 2010. *Tender* is published by Currency Press. Bloom's adaptation of Henrik Ibsen's *Ghosts* was produced by the State Theatre Company of South Australia in October 2008, and is published by Phoenix Press. She jointly adapted Shakespeare's *Romeo and Juliet* with director Geordie Brookman, and this adaptation was first produced by the State Theatre Company of South Australia in August 2010. Additional publications include 'Summer', published by Currency Press in a collection of plays entitled *Short Circuit*, and additional productions include *Summer* by Griffin Theatre Company in 2008, and *Footsoldiers* by Stone/Castro and RealTime Collaborators for Brink's Gorge Festival in 2009.

Bloom's awards include the 2006 Adrian Consett Stephen Memorial Prize (*Tender*), the 2007 Inscription Chairman's Award for Best Play (*Tender*), the 2008 Patrick White Playwrights' Award

(*Bloodwood*), the 2009 Inscription Playwriting Award (*Bloodwood*) and the Henry Lawson Prize for Prose. Her work has also been shortlisted for several awards, including the 2008 New South Wales Premier's Play Award (*Tender*), the 2007 Philip Parsons Playwriting Award (*Tender*), and the 2006 Max Afford Playwriting Award (*Tender*). She has been the recipient of two Goethe Institut scholarships to Germany—the first a language study scholarship in May 2008 and the second to attend Berlin's 'Theatertreffen' as part of an international forum of theatre-makers in May 2009. Bloom was a 2008 Resident Writer at Griffin Theatre Company in Sydney. She is an affiliate artist with Brink Productions in Adelaide and co-artistic director of performance company nowyesnow.

IAIN SINCLAIR is a director, dramaturg and translator with a strong track record in new writing. Since graduating from the RADA masters' program in text and performance studies, Iain has been an active advocate of new writing in theatre as both director and dramaturg. He has produced over thirty new plays in a professional context and has been a dramaturg to many others. Iain has also regularly worked as a director and dramaturg for the ANPC and for PWA. In 2003 Iain took a year studying best practice in developmental dramaturgy, internationally visiting ASK theatre projects in LA, New Dramatists in New York, and the Traverse, Paines Plough, the Royal Court and National Theatre in UK. He is also an established mainstage director whose recent work includes *Our Town*, *Blood Wedding*, *All My Sons* and *Mojo*. His new writing credits include the award-winning original production of Kate Mulvany's *The Seed*, Tom Holloway's *Beyond the Neck*, Donna Abela's *Jump for Jordan* and Eddie Perfect's *The Beast*, as well as premieres of new work by Duncan Graham, Victoria Haralabidou, Caleb Lewis, Mary Rachel Brown and most recently James Millar and Peter Rutherford's new Australian Musical *A Little Touch of Chaos*.

▼ ▼ ▼ ▼ ▼

www.ingramcontent.com/pod-product-compliance
Lightning Source LLC
Chambersburg PA
CBHW050034090426
42735CB00022B/3482